EMILY DICKINSON

# THE POCKET
# EMILY DICKINSON

*Edited by*
BRENDA HILLMAN

SHAMBHALA
*Boston & London*
2009

Shambhala Publications, Inc.
Horticultural Hall
300 Massachusetts Avenue
Boston, Massachusetts 02115

# CONTENTS

# EDITOR'S PREFACE

The first edition of Emily Dickinson's poems I owned was a very skinny paperback with tea stains at the edges of the pages. It had the mythic quality of all of our first inherited paperbacks; we don't know where they come from, but they are old friends by the time they find us. This Emily had some sort of mongrel flower pattern on the cover—at once roses and poppies, but they were dark flowers—and within, fewer than one hundred poems with the pre-1955 bowdlerized punctuation, all the "correct" periods and commas. I realize now, of course, that it was the wrong way to start with Dickinson, but I used to take the little book down into the arroyo—the dry ditch behind the family house—and sit in the eroding dirt, where the dog sniffed around while I read. One poem I read a lot begins: "I started Early—Took my dog— / And visited the Sea / The Mermaids in the Basement / Came out to look at me—." It was the sixties, and was about the time in a life when the issues of identity, the female body, and metaphysics were starting to produce the central questions. This poem is in part about one who travels between nurturing and fear, about how sexual terror and joy may be greeted in outside landscapes as well as in psychological ones, and in part about the activity of the soul in relation to its possible annihilation. It spoke deeply to me, over and over and over.

Because of the importance of this first little paperback to me, the idea of assembling, decades later, a compact, intimate volume of her poems was quite appealing. Emily Dickinson takes up every question about existence we confront. She and Walt Whitman are the spiritual mother and father of American poetry. A look at the subject index to Dickinson's *Complete Poems* edited by Thomas H. Johnson shows that the two largest subject categories are the "Soul" and "Death." This helps explain why contemporary readers still find something rare and strange in her work, and why her poems address everyone: an elderly person struggling with questions of mortality; an adolescent confronting the search for who she is and why she is here; the contemporary artist who may find courage in her formal daring; the traveler—even one who travels for a living—who may find her work the perfect companion because it is so compressed. So the book you hold in your hand could be seen as a guidebook, for exploring the range of human experience.

Of the many reasons to read, or to

reread, Emily Dickinson, three seem important to mention to the general reader. First, read her for that peculiar, strange beauty only she is capable of. It is beauty that doesn't always ask for pure analysis. Opening this book anywhere, you can see that the power of her style comes from compressed excitement. She writes the largest things in the shortest space possible. In dazzling swiftness, we can see her great spirit intercept a question and take it to the interior spaces we didn't know we had. There the poem stays, like a tremendous piece of news dropped down a trap door. The metaphors are always in service of her mind at play, because even when she is deadly serious, she is somehow playful.

Much of the musical beauty in her poems, I find, has to do with breath, with breathlessness. Her poetic rhythms—the use of iambic tetrameter—derive from Protestant hymnals, and are greatly interrupted during the most startling poems by the use of dashes and commas; in the original manuscripts, these appear as hooks, slashes, calligraphic strokes of the pen. Leaving aside the controversial question of whether the quatrains are always quatrains or something else (I will address this in a brief afterword), we can see that the potential solidness or tidiness of the stanzas and the iambic rhythms is made unsafe, precarious, risky by her quirkish punctuation—as if a rope bridge were strung across a raging river far below. The intellectual and physical excitement this creates in the reader is beautiful. A good example occurs in the poem that begins "There's a certain Slant of light":

> Heavenly Hurt, it gives us —
> We can find no scar,
> But internal difference,
> Where the Meanings, are —

This is one of my favorite stanzas. In this poem, winter light, with its oblique Slant, serves as a metaphor for—or rather, it corresponds to—the eternal wound inflicted both outside of and inside a conscious being. The wound and the meaning are in the same place, for Dickinson. I find this stanza amazing partly because of the rhyme of "scar" and "are," and partly because a single comma isolates the "are" at the end of the last line. You must inevitably gulp a bit before reading that word, and slightly gasp afterward. . . . The breath, then, replicates both motion and isolation.

Besides beauty of form, there is the courage of her investigations of human experience. If the contemporary reader notes that she writes with the greatest ease about difficult subjects, it is important to remember that her project has to do with the truth of what people suffer. In a way, she is our first molecular biologist of pain, so that during her period of vast productivity, there are many poems that take one degree (to use one of her favorite words) of the experience of suffering at a time. And since suffering for Dickinson so often has to do with loss, she examines with the most careful lens the relationship between the visible and the invisible realms. First lines like "I felt a Funeral, in my Brain," "'Tis not that Dying hurts us so —" "After great pain, a formal feeling comes —" "Dare you see a Soul *at the White Heat?*" "I heard a Fly buzz — when I died —" and "Pain — has an Element of Blank —" signal these investigations, and one thing we notice right away, if we can give up our prejudice against their "negative subjects," is that these poems are phenomenally stimulating—not in the way a violent movie stimulates, but in the way that seeing our own eyes in the eyes of another is exhilarating and shocking.

And third, although they are occasion-
ally difficult to read, Dickinson's poems
help us to live more purely and with more
power. Because of their epigrammatic
lines, they are infinitely portable. Frag-
ments of these poems can stay in the brain
for a long time, at once familiar and in-
creasingly new. They carry us from com-
fortable to impossible realms within single
lines of their strange diction, and we al-
ways want to figure out how the metaphors
work, so we can repeat them over and over
like mantras. Occasionally when students
tell me it's hard to know how to read the
poems, I tell them, read them quickly and
let them shock you. If a line stays, read it
again until you feel it is yours, and let the
strange capital letters and the dashes carry
the poems to the place in your uncon-
scious that won't worry what they mean.

From 1862 to 1863, between the ages
of thirty-one and thirty-two, Dickinson

drafted over five hundred poems—in one year. Some say Emily Dickinson had fallen in love with a minister who left town, others claim it was with a man who didn't leave town, and still others that she had had a disappointment with a female friend. Most agree—because of their subjects—that the poems were written in a state of extraordinary psychological stress. She had, a year or so earlier, become more and more reclusive. Reading the poems of this period is like watching someone take a long breath and begin to write with her own blood. While the temptation is to seek precise biographical sources for this outpouring, the appropriate response is awe.

The year 1862 is when the monumental losses from the Civil War reached horrendous numbers. Though the battles of Shiloh and Antietam probably did not affect Dickinson's daily life as much as did the deaths from fevers among her neighbors in Amherst, the juxtaposition of these massive casualties from our family war with the breathtakingly intimate work she produced—poems that are at once compact and explosive, grand and interior, in which she explores all the aspects of loss and suffering and remakes her literary persona into a "Queen of Calvary"—is one of our most heartbreaking and compelling American literary paradoxes.

After 1860, Emily Dickinson chose to leave her house only a few times until her death in 1886. What many of us sometimes forget is that she chose one of the few positions of freedom available to her; in fact, given the options for women writers in her day (and the results she achieved), she probably made the only choice available to her. And it's important for us to recall that, even though her choice seems eccentric to contemporary readers, she was also the middle, responsible daughter of a very busy household, very much a caretaker for family and servants. We have, besides her voluminous poems and letters, inherited some of her recipes, notably one for gingerbread; it makes a very large quantity.

Other facts of her life are relatively simple. Born in Amherst in 1830, the middle child of a prominent lawyer, she went away to Mount Holyoke Seminary for one year only. Her older brother's marriage to her close (and temperamental) friend Susan Gilbert occurred in 1856, and shortly thereafter Dickinson began to write poems that she would later assemble into packets or fascicles, little manuscript books tacked together with thread, which is how her sister Lavinia found them after her death. The crisis she experienced in the early 1860s remains a mystery, though much has been conjectured about the one to whom her love poems are addressed and the intended recipient of the famous "Master" letters, drafts of which were also found in her desk. We do know that when she finally sent some of her poems "to the world" outside her family and friends, it was to a Boston man of letters named Thomas Wentworth Higginson, and that she asked him whether her verses "breathed." It was probably immediately apparent to her that Higginson wouldn't be a helpful critic, but she wrote to him anyway, often astonishing and entertaining letters. Otherwise, she requested advice from only a few friends. With the exception of a few dozen poems, Dickinson was the only reader of the more than seventeen hundred poems she produced. She died of Bright's disease, a debilitating kidney disorder. The inscription on her tombstone is a quote from her last "letter to the world"; it reads simply: "Called Home."

A few words about my selection process in this little volume: I chose the poems I've loved the best, and a few I learned to love in rereading Dickinson's complete work. I've tried to represent the range of her vision. I am indebted to Robert Hass, Stephen Mitchell, and Peter Turner for their suggestions and advice.

# THE POCKET
# EMILY DICKINSON

A Day! Help! Help! Another Day!
Your prayers, oh Passer by!
From such a common ball as this
Might date a Victory!
From marshallings as simple
The flags of nations swang.
Steady — my soul: What issues
Upon thine arrow hang!

c. 1858

I NEVER lost as much but twice,
And that was in the sod.
Twice have I stood a beggar
Before the door of God!

Angels — twice descending
Reimbursed my store —
Burglar! Banker — Father!
I am poor once more!

c. 1858

Success is counted sweetest
By those who ne'er succeed.
To comprehend a nectar
Requires sorest need.

Not one of all the purple Host
Who took the Flag today
Can tell the definition
So clear of Victory

As he defeated – dying –
On whose forbidden ear
The distant strains of triumph
Burst agonized and clear!

c. 1859

Low at my problem bending,
Another problem comes —
Larger than mine — Serener —
Involving statelier sums.

I check my busy pencil,
My figures file away.
Wherefore, my baffled fingers
Thy perplexity?

c. 1859

Our lives are Swiss —
So still — so Cool —
Till some odd afternoon
The Alps neglect their Curtains
And we look farther on!

*Italy* stands the other side!
While like a guard between —
The solemn Alps —
The siren Alps
Forever intervene!

c. 1859

ONE dignity delays for all —
One mitred Afternoon —
None can avoid this purple —
None evade this Crown!

Coach, it insures, and footmen —
Chamber, and state, and throng —
Bells, also, in the village
As we ride grand along!

What dignified Attendants!
What service when we pause!
How loyally at parting
Their hundred hats they raise!

How pomp surpassing ermine
When simple You, and I,
Present our meek escutcheon
And claim the rank to die!

c. 1859

WILL there really be a "Morning"?
Is there such a thing as "Day"?
Could I see it from the mountains
If I were as tall as they?

Has it feet like Water lilies?
Has it feathers like a Bird?
Is it brought from famous countries
Of which I have never heard?

Oh some Scholar! Oh some Sailor!
Oh some Wise Man from the skies!
Please to tell a little Pilgrim
Where the place called "Morning" lies!

c. 1859

These are the days when Birds come
    back –
A very few – a Bird or two –
To take a backward look.

These are the days when skies resume
The old – old sophistries of June –
A blue and gold mistake.

Oh fraud that cannot cheat the Bee –
Almost thy plausibility
Induces my belief.

Till ranks of seeds their witness bear –
And softly thro' the altered air
Hurries a timid leaf.

Oh Sacrament of summer days,
Oh Last Communion in the Haze –
Permit a child to join.

Thy sacred emblems to partake —
Thy consecrated bread to take
And thine immortal wine!

c. 1859

To fight aloud, is very brave –
But *gallanter,* I know
Who charge within the bosom
The Cavalry of Woe –

Who win, and nations do not see –
Who fall – and none observe –
Whose dying eyes, no Country
Regards with patriot love –

We trust, in plumed procession
For such, the Angels go –
Rank after Rank, with even feet –
And Uniforms of Snow.

c. 1859

How many times these low feet
   staggered –
Only the soldered mouth can tell –
Try – can you stir the awful rivet –
Try – can you lift the hasps of steel!

Stroke the cool forehead – hot so often –
Lift – if you care – the listless hair –
Handle the adamantine fingers
Never a thimble – more – shall wear –

Buzz the dull flies – on the chamber
   window –
Brave – shines the sun through the
   freckled pane –
Fearless – the cobweb swings from
   the ceiling –
Indolent Housewife – in Daisies – lain!

c. 1860

I SHALL know why — when Time is
    over —
And I have ceased to wonder why —
Christ will explain each separate anguish
In the fair schoolroom of the sky —

He will tell me what "Peter" promised —
And I — for wonder at his woe —
I shall forget the drop of Anguish
That scalds me now — that scalds me now!

c. 1860

I'M "wife" — I've finished that —
That other state —
I'm Czar — I'm "Woman" now —
It's safer so —

How odd the Girl's life looks
Behind this soft Eclipse —
I think that Earth feels so
To folks in Heaven — now —

This being comfort — then
That other kind — was pain —
But why compare?
I'm "Wife"! Stop there!

c. 1860

I TASTE a liquor never brewed –
From Tankards scooped in Pearl –
Not all the Vats upon the Rhine
Yield such an Alcohol!

Inebriate of Air – am I –
And Debauchee of Dew –
Reeling – thro endless summer days –
From inns of Molten Blue –

When "Landlords" turn the drunken
    Bee
Out of the Foxglove's door –
When Butterflies – renounce their
    "drams" –
I shall but drink the more!

Till Seraphs swing their snowy Hats —
And Saints — to windows run —
To see the little Tippler
Leaning against the — Sun —

c. 1860

Safe in their Alabaster Chambers —
Untouched by Morning —
And untouched by Noon —
Lie the meek members of the
    Resurrection —
Rafter of Satin — and Roof of Stone!

Grand go the Years — in the Crescent —
    above them —
Worlds scoop their Arcs —
And Firmaments — row —
Diadems — drop — and Doges —
    surrender —
Soundless as dots — on a Disc of Snow —

*version of* 1861

SHE sweeps with many-colored Brooms —
And leaves the Shreds behind —
Oh Housewife in the Evening West —
Come back, and dust the Pond!

You dropped a Purple Ravelling in —
You dropped an Amber thread —
And now you've littered all the East
With Duds of Emerald!

And still, she plies her spotted Brooms,
And still the Aprons fly,
Till Brooms fade softly into stars —
And then I come away —

c. 1861

SHOULD you but fail at – Sea –
In sight of me –
Or doomed lie –
Next Sun – to die –
Or rap – at Paradise – unheard
I'd *harass God*
Until he let you in!

1861

THE Lamp burns sure – within –
Tho' Serfs – supply the Oil –
It matters not the busy Wick –
At her phosphoric toil!

The Slave – forgets – to fill –
The Lamp – burns golden – on –
Unconscious that the oil is out –
As that the Slave – is gone.

c. 1861

I LIKE a look of Agony,
Because I know it's true —
Men do not sham Convulsion,
Nor simulate, a Throe —

The Eyes glaze once — and that is Death —
Impossible to feign
The Beads upon the Forehead
By homely Anguish strung.

c. 1861

I⊤ is easy to work when the soul is at
     play –
But when the soul is in pain –
The hearing him put his playthings up
Makes work difficult – then –

It is simple, to ache in the Bone, or the
     Rind –
But Gimlets – among the nerve –
Mangle daintier – terribler –
Like a Panther in the Glove –

c. 1861

WILD Nights – Wild Nights!
Were I with thee
Wild Nights should be
Our luxury!

Futile – the Winds –
To a Heart in port –
Done with the Compass –
Done with the Chart!

Rowing in Eden –
Ah, the Sea!
Might I but moor – Tonight –
In Thee!

c. 1861

I CAN wade Grief —
Whole Pools of it —
I'm used to that —
But the least push of Joy
Breaks up my feet —
And I tip — drunken —
Let no Pebble — smile —
'Twas the New Liquor —
That was all!

Power is only Pain —
Stranded, thro' Discipline,
Till Weights — will hang —
Give Balm — to Giants —
And they'll wilt, like Men —
Give Himmaleh —
They'll Carry — Him!

c. 1861

"Hope" is the thing with feathers –
That perches in the soul –
And sings the tune without the words –
And never stops – at all –

And sweetest – in the Gale – is heard –
And sore must be the storm –
That could abash the little Bird
That kept so many warm –

I've heard it in the chillest land –
And on the strangest Sea –
Yet, never, in Extremity,
It asked a crumb – of Me.

c. 1861

There's a certain Slant of light,
Winter Afternoons —
That oppresses, like the Heft
Of Cathedral Tunes —

Heavenly Hurt, it gives us —
We can find no scar,
But internal difference,
Where the Meanings, are —

None may teach it — Any —
'Tis the Seal Despair —
An imperial affliction
Sent us of the Air —

When it comes, the Landscape listens —
Shadows — hold their breath —
When it goes, 'tis like the Distance
On the look of Death —

c. 1861

I FELT a Funeral, in my Brain,
And Mourners to and fro
Kept treading – treading – till it seemed
That Sense was breaking through –

And when they all were seated,
A Service, like a Drum –
Kept beating – beating – till I thought
My Mind was going numb –

And then I heard them lift a Box
And creak across my Soul
With those same Boots of Lead, again,
Then Space – began to toll,

As all the Heavens were a Bell,
And Being, but an Ear,
And I, and silence, some strange Race
Wrecked, solitary, here –

And then a Plank in Reason, broke,
And I dropped down, and down —
And hit a World, at every plunge,
And Finished knowing — then —

c. 1861

A SOLEMN thing – it was – I said –
A woman – white – to be –
And wear – if God should count me fit –
Her blameless mystery –

A hallowed thing – to drop a life
Into the purple well –
Too plummetless – that it return –
Eternity – until –

I pondered how the bliss would look –
And would it feel as big –
When I could take it in my hand –
As hovering – seen – through fog –

And then – the size of this "small" life –
The Sages – call it small –
Swelled – like Horizons – in my vest –
And I sneered – softly – "small"!

c. 1861

I'm Nobody! Who are you?
Are you – Nobody – Too?
Then there's a pair of us!
Don't tell! they'd advertise – you know!

How dreary – to be – Somebody!
How public – like a Frog –
To tell one's name – the livelong June –
To an admiring Bog!

c. 1861

A Clock stopped –
Not the Mantel's –
Geneva's farthest skill
Can't put the puppet bowing –
That just now dangled still –

An awe came on the Trinket!
The Figures hunched, with pain –
Then quivered out of Decimals –
Into Degreeless Noon –

It will not stir for Doctors –
This Pendulum of snow –
This Shopman importunes it –
While cool – concernless No –

Nods from the Gilded pointers –
Nods from the Seconds slim –

Decades of Arrogance between
The Dial life —
And Him —

c. 1861

IF your Nerve, deny you —
Go above your Nerve —
He can lean against the Grave,
If he fear to swerve —

That's a steady posture —
Never any bend
Held of those Brass arms —
Best Giant made —

If your Soul seesaw —
Lift the Flesh door —
The Poltroon wants Oxygen —
Nothing more —

c. 1861

THE Soul selects her own Society —
Then — shuts the Door —
To her divine Majority —
Present no more —

Unmoved — she notes the Chariots —
   pausing —
At her low Gate —
Unmoved — an Emperor be kneeling
Upon her Mat —

I've known her — from an ample nation —
Choose One —
Then — close the Valves of her attention —
Like Stone —

c. 1862

THE difference between Despair
And Fear — is like the One
Between the instant of a Wreck —
And when the Wreck has been —

The Mind is smooth — no Motion —
Contented as the Eye
Upon the Forehead of a Bust —
That knows — it cannot see —

c. 1862

He fumbles at your Soul
As Players at the Keys
Before they drop full Music on —
He stuns you by degrees —
Prepares your brittle Nature
For the Ethereal Blow
By fainter Hammers — further heard —
Then nearer — Then so slow
Your Breath has time to straighten —
Your Brain — to bubble Cool —
Deals — One — imperial — Thunderbolt —
That scalps your naked Soul —

When Winds take Forests in their Paws —
The Universe — is still —

c. 1862

SOME keep the Sabbath going to
 Church —
I keep it, staying at Home —
With a Bobolink for a Chorister —
And an Orchard, for a Dome —

Some keep the Sabbath in Surplice —
I just wear my Wings —
And instead of tolling the Bell, for Church,
Our little Sexton — sings.

God preaches, a noted Clergyman —
And the sermon is never long,
So instead of getting to Heaven, at last —
I'm going, all along.

c. 1860

'Tis not that Dying hurts us so —
'Tis Living — hurts us more —
But Dying — is a different way —
A Kind behind the Door —

The Southern Custom — of the Bird —
That ere the Frosts are due —
Accepts a better Latitude —
We — are the Birds — that stay.

The Shiverers round Farmers' doors —
For whose reluctant Crumb —
We stipulate — till pitying Snows
Persuade our Feathers Home.

c. 1862

Before I got my eye put out
I liked as well to see —
As other Creatures, that have Eyes
And know no other way —

But were it told to me — Today —
That I might have the sky
For mine — I tell you that my Heart
Would split, for size of me —

The Meadows — mine —
The Mountains — mine —
All Forests — Stintless Stars —
As much of Noon as I could take
Between my finite eyes —

The Motions of the Dipping Birds —
The Morning's Amber Road —
For mine — to look at when I liked —
The News would strike me dead —

So safer – guess – with just my soul
Upon the Window pane –
Where other Creatures put their eyes –
Incautious – of the Sun –

c. 1862

A BIRD came down the Walk —
He did not know I saw —
He bit an Angleworm in halves
And ate the fellow, raw,

And then he drank a Dew
From a convenient Grass —
And then hopped sidewise to the Wall
To let a Beetle pass —

He glanced with rapid eyes
That hurried all around —
They looked like frightened Beads, I
    thought —
He stirred his Velvet Head

Like one in danger, Cautious,
I offered him a Crumb
And he unrolled his feathers
And rowed him softer home —

Than Oars divide the Ocean,
Too silver for a seam —
Or Butterflies, off Banks of Noon
Leap, plashless as they swim.

c. 1862

I KNOW that He exists.
Somewhere – in Silence –
He has hid his rare life
From our gross eyes.

'Tis an instant's play.
'Tis a fond Ambush –
Just to make Bliss
Earn her own surprise!

But – should the play
Prove piercing earnest –
Should the glee – glaze –
In Death's – stiff – stare –

Would not the fun
Look too expensive!
Would not the jest –
Have crawled too far!

c. 1862

AFTER great pain, a formal feeling
  comes —
The Nerves sit ceremonious, like Tombs —
The stiff Heart questions was it He, that
  bore,
And Yesterday, or Centuries before?

The Feet, mechanical, go round —
Of Ground, or Air, or Ought —
A Wooden way
Regardless grown,
A Quartz contentment, like a stone —

This is the Hour of Lead —
Remembered, if outlived,
As Freezing persons, recollect the Snow —
First — Chill — then Stupor — then the
  letting go —

c. 1862

I DREADED that first Robin, so,
But He is mastered, now,
I'm some accustomed to Him grown,
He hurts a little, though —

I thought if I could only live
Till that first Shout got by —
Not all Pianos in the Woods
Had power to mangle me —

I dared not meet the Daffodils —
For fear their Yellow Gown
Would pierce me with a fashion
So foreign to my own —

I wished the Grass would hurry —
So — when 'twas time to see —
He'd be too tall, the tallest one
Could stretch — to look at me —

I could not bear the Bees should come,
I wished they'd stay away
In those dim countries where they go,
What word had they, for me?

They're here, though; not a creature
    failed –
No Blossom stayed away
In gentle deference to me –
The Queen of Calvary –

Each one salutes me, as he goes,
And I, my childish Plumes,
Lift, in bereaved acknowledgment
Of their unthinking Drums –

c. 1862

Funny — to be a Century —
And see the People — going by —
I — should die of the Oddity —
But then — I'm not so staid — as He —

He keeps His Secrets safely — very —
Were He to tell — extremely sorry
This Bashful Globe of Ours would be —
So dainty of Publicity —

c. 1862

DARE you see a Soul *at the White Heat?*
Then crouch within the door —
Red — is the Fire's common tint —
But when the vivid Ore
Has vanquished Flame's conditions,
It quivers from the Forge
Without a color, but the light
Of unanointed Blaze.
Least Village has its Blacksmith
Whose Anvil's even ring
Stands symbol for the finer Forge
That soundless tugs — within —
Refining these impatient Ores
With Hammer, and with Blaze
Until the Designated Light
Repudiate the Forge —

c. 1862

OF Course – I prayed –
And did God Care?
He cared as much as on the Air
A Bird – had stamped her foot –
And cried "Give Me" –
My Reason – Life –
I had not had – but for Yourself –
'Twere better Charity
To leave me in the Atom's Tomb –
Merry, and Nought, and gay, and numb –
Than this smart Misery.

c. 1862

Dɪᴅ Our Best Moment last –
'Twould supersede the Heaven –
A few – and they by Risk – procure –
So this Sort – are not given –

Except as stimulants – in
Cases of Despair –
Or Stupor – The Reserve –
These Heavenly Moments are –

A Grant of the Divine –
That Certain as it Comes –
Withdraws – and leaves the dazzled Soul
In her unfurnished Rooms

c. 1862

THE first Day's Night had come –
And grateful that a thing
So terrible – had been endured –
I told my Soul to sing –

She said her Strings were snapt –
Her Bow – to Atoms blown –
And so to mend her – gave me work
Until another Morn –

And then – a Day as huge
As Yesterdays in pairs,
Unrolled its horror in my face –
Until it blocked my eyes –

My Brain – begun to laugh –
I mumbled – like a fool –
And tho' 'tis Years ago – that Day –
My Brain keeps giggling – still.

And Something's odd – within –
That person that I was –
And this One – do not feel the same –
Could it be Madness – this?

c. 1862

'Twas like a Maelstrom, with a notch,
That nearer, every Day,
Kept narrowing its boiling Wheel
Until the Agony

Toyed coolly with the final inch
Of your delirious Hem —
And you dropt, lost,
When something broke —
And let you from a Dream —

As if a Goblin with a Gauge —
Kept measuring the Hours —
Until you felt your Second
Weigh, helpless, in his Paws —

And not a Sinew — stirred — could help,
And sense was setting numb —
When God — remembered — and the Fiend
Let go, then, Overcome —

As if your Sentence stood – pronounced –
And you were frozen led
From Dungeon's luxury of Doubt
To Gibbets, and the Dead –

And when the Film had stitched your eyes
A Creature gasped "Reprieve"!
Which Anguish was the utterest – then –
To perish, or to live?

c. 1862

It might be lonelier
Without the Loneliness –
I'm so accustomed to my Fate –
Perhaps the Other – Peace –

Would interrupt the Dark –
And crowd the little Room –
Too scant – by Cubits – to contain
The Sacrament – of Him –

I am not used to Hope –
It might intrude upon –
Its sweet parade – blaspheme the place –
Ordained to Suffering –

It might be easier
To fail – with Land in Sight –
Than gain – My Blue Peninsula –
To perish – of Delight –

c. 1862

Not in this World to see his face –
Sounds long – until I read the place
Where this – is said to be
But just the Primer – to a life –
Unopened – rare – Upon the Shelf –
Clasped yet – to Him – and me –

And yet – My Primer suits me so
I would not choose – a Book to know
Than that – be sweeter wise –
Might some one else – so learned – be –
And leave me – just my A – B – C –
Himself – could have the Skies –

c. 1862

WE grow accustomed to the Dark —
When Light is put away —
As when the Neighbor holds the Lamp
To witness her Goodbye —

A Moment — We uncertain step
For newness of the night —
Then — fit our Vision to the Dark —
And meet the Road — erect —

And so of larger — Darknesses —
Those Evenings of the Brain —
When not a Moon disclose a sign —
Or Star — come out — within —

The Bravest — grope a little —
And sometimes hit a Tree
Directly in the Forehead —
But as they learn to see —

Either the Darkness alters —
Or something in the sight
Adjusts itself to Midnight —
And Life steps almost straight.

c. 1862

MUCH Madness is divinest Sense —
To a discerning Eye —
Much Sense — the starkest Madness —
'Tis the Majority
In this, as All, prevail —
Assent — and you are sane —
Demur — you're straightway dangerous —
And handled with a Chain —

c. 1862

This is my letter to the World
That never wrote to Me —
The simple News that Nature told —
With tender Majesty

Her Message is committed
To Hands I cannot see —
For love of Her — Sweet — countrymen —
Judge tenderly — of Me

c. 1862

I DIED for Beauty – but was scarce
Adjusted in the Tomb
When One who died for Truth, was lain
In an adjoining Room –

He questioned softly "Why I failed"?
"For Beauty", I replied –
"And I – for Truth – Themself are One –
We Brethren, are", He said –

And so, as Kinsmen, met a Night –
We talked between the Rooms –
Until the Moss had reached our lips –
And covered up – our names –

c. 1862

THE Outer — from the Inner
Derives its Magnitude —
'Tis Duke, or Dwarf, according
As is the Central Mood —

The fine — unvarying Axis
That regulates the Wheel —
Though Spokes — spin — more conspicuous
And fling a dust — the while.

The Inner — paints the Outer —
The Brush without the Hand —
Its Picture publishes — precise —
As is the inner Brand —

On fine — Arterial Canvas —
A Cheek — perchance a Brow —
The Star's whole Secret — in the Lake —
Eyes were not meant to know.

c. 1862

I LIVE with Him — I see His face —
I go no more away
For Visitor — or Sundown —
Death's single privacy

The Only One — forestalling Mine —
And that — by Right that He
Presents a Claim invisible —
No wedlock — granted Me —

I live with Him — I hear His Voice —
I stand alive — Today —
To witness to the Certainty
Of Immortality —

Taught Me — by Time — the lower Way —
Conviction — Every day —
That Life like This — is stopless —
Be Judgment — what it may —

c. 1862

I HEARD a Fly buzz – when I died –
The Stillness in the Room
Was like the Stillness in the Air –
Between the Heaves of Storm –

The Eyes around – had wrung them dry –
And Breaths were gathering firm
For that last Onset – when the King
Be witnessed – in the Room –

I willed my Keepsakes – Signed away
What portion of me be
Assignable – and then it was
There interposed a Fly –

With Blue – uncertain stumbling Buzz –
Between the light – and me –
And then the Windows failed – and then
I could not see to see –

c. 1862

I ENVY Seas, whereon He rides —
I envy Spokes of Wheels
Of Chariots, that Him convey —
I envy Crooked Hills

That gaze upon His journey —
How easy All can see
What is forbidden utterly
As Heaven — unto me!

I envy Nests of Sparrows —
That dot His distant Eaves —
The wealthy Fly, upon His Pane —
The happy — happy Leaves —

That just abroad His Window
Have Summer's leave to play —
The Ear Rings of Pizarro
Could not obtain for me —

I envy Light — that wakes Him —
And Bells — that boldly ring
To tell Him it is Noon, abroad —
Myself — be Noon to Him —

Yet interdict — my Blossom —
And abrogate — my Bee —
Lest Noon in Everlasting Night —
Drop Gabriel — and Me —

c. 1862

WITHIN my Garden, rides a Bird
Upon a single Wheel —
Whose spokes a dizzy Music make
As 'twere a travelling Mill —

He never stops, but slackens
Above the Ripest Rose —
Partakes without alighting
And praises as he goes,

Till every spice is tasted —
And then his Fairy Gig
Reels in remoter atmospheres —
And I rejoin my Dog,

And He and I, perplex us
If positive, 'twere we —
Or bore the Garden in the Brain
This Curiosity —

But He, the best Logician,
Refers my clumsy eye —
To just vibrating Blossoms!
An Exquisite Reply!

c. 1862

THIS World is not Conclusion.
A Species stands beyond —
Invisible, as Music —
But positive, as Sound —
It beckons, and it baffles —
Philosophy — don't know —
And through a Riddle, at the last —
Sagacity, must go —
To guess it, puzzles scholars —
To gain it, Men have borne
Contempt of Generations
And Crucifixion, shown —
Faith slips — and laughs, and rallies —
Blushes, if any see —
Plucks at a twig of Evidence —
And asks a Vane, the way —

Much Gesture, from the Pulpit —
Strong Hallelujahs roll —
Narcotics cannot still the Tooth
That nibbles at the soul —

c. 1862

I'm ceded – I've stopped being Theirs –
The name They dropped upon my face
With water, in the country church
Is finished using, now,
And They can put it with my Dolls,
My childhood, and the string of spools,
I've finished threading – too –

Baptized, before, without the choice,
But this time, consciously, of Grace –
Unto supremest name –
Called to my Full – The Crescent
    dropped –
Existence's whole Arc, filled up,
With one small Diadem.

My second Rank – too small the first –
Crowned – Crowing – on my Father's
    breast –
A half unconscious Queen –

But this time — Adequate — Erect,
With Will to choose, or to reject,
And I choose, just a Crown —

c. 1862

It was not Death, for I stood up,
And all the Dead, lie down —
It was not Night, for all the Bells
Put out their Tongues, for Noon.

It was not Frost, for on my Flesh
I felt Siroccos — crawl —
Nor Fire — for just my Marble feet
Could keep a Chancel, cool —

And yet, it tasted, like them all,
The Figures I have seen
Set orderly, for Burial,
Reminded me, of mine —

As if my life were shaven,
And fitted to a frame,
And could not breathe without a key,
And 'twas like Midnight, some —

When everything that ticked — has
    stopped —
And Space stares all around —
Or Grisly frosts — first Autumn morns,
Repeal the Beating Ground —

But, most, like Chaos — Stopless — cool —
Without a Chance, or Spar —
Or even a Report of Land —
To justify — Despair.

c. 1862

THE Soul has Bandaged moments –
When too appalled to stir –
She feels some ghastly Fright come up
And stop to look at her –

Salute her – with long fingers –
Caress her freezing hair –
Sip, Goblin, from the very lips
The Lover – hovered – o'er –
Unworthy, that a thought so mean
Accost a Theme – so – fair –

The soul has moments of Escape –
When bursting all the doors –
She dances like a Bomb, abroad,
And swings upon the Hours,

As do the Bee – delirious borne –
Long Dungeoned from his Rose –

Touch Liberty — then know no more,
But Noon, and Paradise —

The Soul's retaken moments —
When, Felon led along,
With shackles on the plumed feet,
And staples, in the Song,

The Horror welcomes her, again,
These, are not brayed of Tongue —

c. 1862

I started Early – Took my Dog –
And visited the Sea –
The Mermaids in the Basement
Came out to look at me –

And Frigates – in the Upper Floor
Extended Hempen Hands –
Presuming Me to be a Mouse –
Aground – upon the Sands –

But no Man moved Me – till the Tide
Went past my simple Shoe –
And past my Apron – and my Belt
And past my Bodice – too –

And made as He would eat me up –
As wholly as a Dew
Upon a Dandelion's Sleeve –
And then – I started – too –

And He – He followed – close behind –
I felt His Silver Heel
Upon my Ankle – Then my Shoes
Would overflow with Pearl –

Until We met the Solid Town –
No One He seemed to know –
And bowing – with a Mighty look –
At me – The Sea withdrew –

c. 1862

No Man can compass a Despair —
As round a Goalless Road
No faster than a Mile at once
The Traveller proceed —

Unconscious of the Width —
Unconscious that the Sun
Be setting on His progress —
So accurate the One

At estimating Pain —
Whose own — has just begun —
His ignorance — the Angel
That pilot Him along —

c. 1862

MINE — by the Right of the White Election!
Mine — by the Royal Seal!
Mine — by the Sign in the Scarlet prison —
Bars — cannot conceal!

Mine — here — in Vision — and in Veto!
Mine — by the Grave's Repeal —
Titled — Confirmed —
Delirious Charter!
Mine — long as Ages steal!

c. 1862

THE Heart asks Pleasure – first –
And then – Excuse from Pain –
And then – those little Anodynes
That deaden suffering –

And then – to go to sleep –
And then – if it should be
The will of its Inquisitor
The privilege to die –

c. 1862

To fill a Gap
Insert the Thing that caused it —
Block it up
With Other — and 'twill yawn the more —
You cannot solder an Abyss
With Air.

c. 1862

I've seen a Dying Eye
Run round and round a Room —
In search of Something — as it seemed —
Then Cloudier become —
And then — obscure with Fog —
And then — be soldered down
Without disclosing what it be
'Twere blessed to have seen —

c. 1862

I MEASURE every Grief I meet
With narrow, probing, Eyes —
I wonder if It weighs like Mine —
Or has an Easier size.

I wonder if They bore it long —
Or did it just begin —
I could not tell the Date of Mine —
It feels so old a pain —

I wonder if it hurts to live —
And if They have to try —
And whether — could They choose
    between —
It would not be — to die —

I note that Some — gone patient long —
At length, renew their smile —
An imitation of a Light
That has so little Oil —

I wonder if when Years have piled —
Some Thousands — on the Harm —
That hurt them early — such a lapse
Could give them any Balm —

Or would they go on aching still
Through Centuries of Nerve —
Enlightened to a larger Pain —
In Contrast with the Love —

The Grieved — are many — I am told —
There is the various Cause —
Death — is but one — and comes but
    once —
And only nails the eyes —

There's Grief of Want — and Grief of
    Cold —
A sort they call "Despair" —
There's Banishment from native Eyes —
In sight of Native Air —

And though I may not guess the kind –
Correctly – yet to me
A piercing Comfort it affords
In passing Calvary –

To note the fashions – of the Cross –
And how they're mostly worn –
Still fascinated to presume
That Some – are like My Own –

c. 1862

I COULD not prove the Years had feet –
Yet confident they run
Am I, from symptoms that are past
And Series that are done –

I find my feet have further Goals –
I smile upon the Aims
That felt so ample – Yesterday –
Today's – have vaster claims –

I do not doubt the self I was
Was competent to me –
But something awkward in the fit –
Proves that – outgrown – I see –

c. 1862

I RECKON — when I count at all —
First — Poets — Then the Sun —
Then Summer — Then the Heaven of God —
then — the List is done —

But, looking back — the First so seems
To Comprehend the Whole —
The Others look a needless Show —
So I write — Poets — All —

Their Summer — lasts a Solid Year —
They can afford a Sun
The East — would deem extravagant —
And if the Further Heaven —

Be Beautiful as they prepare
For Those who worship Them —
It is too difficult a Grace —
To justify the Dream —

c. 1862

I HAD been hungry, all the Years —
My Noon had Come — to dine —
I trembling drew the Table near —
And touched the Curious Wine —

'Twas this on Tables I had seen —
When turning, hungry, Home
I looked in Windows, for the Wealth
I could not hope — for Mine —

I did not know the ample Bread —
'Twas so unlike the Crumb
The Birds and I, had often shared
In Nature's — Dining Room —

The Plenty hurt me — 'twas so new —
Myself felt ill — and odd —
As Berry — of a Mountain Bush —
Transplanted — to the Road —

Nor was I hungry — so I found
That Hunger — was a way
Of Persons outside Windows —
The Entering — takes away —

c. 1862

I LIKE to see it lap the Miles —
And lick the Valleys up —
And stop to feed itself at Tanks —
And then — prodigious step

Around a Pile of Mountains —
And supercilious peer
In Shanties — by the sides of Roads —
And then a Quarry pare

To fit its Ribs
And crawl between
Complaining all the while
In horrid — hooting stanza —
Then chase itself down Hill —

And neigh like Boanerges —
Then — punctual as a Star
Stop — docile and omnipotent
At its own stable door —

c. 1862

THERE is a pain – so utter –
It swallows substance up –
Then covers the Abyss with Trance –
So Memory can step
Around – across – upon it –
As one within a Swoon –
Goes safely – where an open eye –
Would drop Him – Bone by Bone.

c. 1862

I Years had been from Home
And now before the Door
I dared not enter, lest a Face
I never saw before

Stare stolid into mine
And ask my Business there –
"My Business but a Life I left
Was such remaining there?"

I leaned upon the Awe –
I lingered with Before –
The Second like an Ocean rolled
And broke against my ear –

I laughed a crumbling Laugh
That I could fear a Door
Who Consternation compassed
And never winced before.

I fitted to the Latch
My Hand, with trembling care
Lest back the awful Door should spring
And leave me in the Floor —

Then moved my Fingers off
As cautiously as Glass
And held my ears, and like a Thief
Fled gasping from the House —

c. 1872
from an 1862 version

I SEE thee better – in the Dark –
I do not need a Light –
The Love of Thee – a Prism be –
Excelling Violet –

I see thee better for the Years
That hunch themselves between –
The Miner's Lamp – sufficient be –
To nullify the Mine –

And in the Grave – I see Thee best –
Its little Panels be
Aglow – All ruddy – with the Light
I held so high, for Thee –

What need of Day –
To Those whose Dark – hath so –
    surpassing Sun –

It deem it be – Continually –
At the Meridian?

c. 1862

IT would have starved a Gnat —
To live so small as I —
And yet I was a living Child —
With Food's necessity

Upon me — like a Claw —
I could no more remove
Than I could coax a Leech away —
Or make a Dragon — move —

Nor like the Gnat — had I —
The privilege to fly
And seek a Dinner for myself —
How mightier He — than I —

Nor like Himself — the Art
Upon the Window Pane
To gad my little Being out —
And not begin — again —

c. 1862

THEY shut me up in Prose –
As when a little Girl
They put me in the Closet –
Because they liked me "still" –

Still! Could themself have peeped –
And seen my Brain – go round –
They might as wise have lodged a Bird
For Treason – in the Pound –

Himself has but to will
And easy as a Star
Abolish his Captivity –
And laugh – No more have I –

c. 1862

I cannot live with You —
It would be Life —
And Life is over there —
Behind the Shelf

The Sexton keeps the Key to —
Putting up
Our Life — His Porcelain —
Like a Cup —

Discarded of the Housewife —
Quaint — or Broke —
A newer Sevres pleases —
Old Ones crack —

I could not die — with You —
For One must wait
To shut the Other's Gaze down —
You — could not —

And I – Could I stand by
And see You – freeze –
Without my Right of Frost –
Death's privilege?

Nor could I rise – with You –
Because Your Face
Would put out Jesus' –
That New Grace

Glow plain – and foreign
On my homesick Eye –
Except that You than He
Shone closer by –

They'd judge Us – How –
For You – served Heaven – You know,
Or sought to –
I could not –

Because You saturated Sight –
And I had no more Eyes

For sordid excellence
As Paradise

And were You lost, I would be —
Though My Name
Rang loudest
On the Heavenly fame —

And were You — saved —
And I — condemned to be
Where You were not —
That self — were Hell to Me —

So We must meet apart —
You there — I — here —
With just the Door ajar
That Oceans are — and Prayer —
And that White Sustenance —
Despair —

c. 1862

THE Brain — is wider than the Sky —
For — put them side by side —
The one the other will contain
With ease — and You — beside —

The Brain is deeper than the sea —
For — hold them — Blue to Blue —
The one the other will absorb —
As Sponges — Buckets — do —

The Brain is just the weight of God —
For — Heft them — Pound for Pound —
And they will differ — if they do —
As Syllable from Sound —

c. 1862

I THINK to Live — may be a Bliss
To those who dare to try —
Beyond my limit to conceive —
My lip — to testify —

I think the Heart I former wore
Could widen — till to me
The Other, like the little Bank
Appear — unto the Sea —

I think the Days — could every one
In Ordination stand —
And Majesty — be easier —
Than an inferior kind —

No numb alarm — lest Difference come —
No Goblin — on the Bloom —
No start in Apprehension's Ear,
No Bankruptcy — no Doom —

But Certainties of Sun —
Midsummer — in the Mind —
A steadfast South — upon the Soul —
Her Polar time — behind —

The Vision — pondered long —
So plausible becomes
That I esteem the fiction — real —
The Real — fictitious seems —

How bountiful the Dream —
What Plenty — it would be —
Had all my Life but been Mistake
Just rectified — in Thee

c. 1862

P<small>AIN</small> — has an Element of Blank —
It cannot recollect
When it begun — or if there were
A time when it was not —

It has no Future — but itself —
Its Infinite contain
Its past — enlightened to perceive
New Periods — of Pain.

c. 1862

I DWELL in Possibility —
A fairer House than Prose —
More numerous of Windows —
Superior — for Doors —

Of Chambers as the Cedars —
Impregnable of Eye —
And for an Everlasting Roof
The Gambrels of the Sky —

Of Visitors — the fairest —
For Occupation — This —
The spreading wide my narrow Hands
To gather Paradise —

c. 1862

AGAIN – his voice is at the door –
I feel the old *Degree* –
I hear him ask the servant
For such an one – as me –

I take a *flower* – as I go –
My face to *justify* –
He never *saw* me – *in this life* –
I might *surprise* his eye!

I cross the Hall with *mingled* steps –
I – silent – pass the door –
I look on all this world *contains* –
*Just his face* – nothing more!

We talk in *careless* – and in *toss* –
A kind of *plummet* strain –
Each – sounding – shyly –
Just – how – deep –
The *other's* one – had been –

We *walk* – I leave my Dog – at home –
A *tender* – *thoughtful* Moon
Goes with us – just a little way –
And – then – we are *alone* –

*Alone* – if *Angels* are "alone" –
*First time* they *try* the *sky*!
*Alone* – if those "veiled faces" – be –
We cannot *count* – on High!

I'd give – to live that hour – *again* –
The *purple* – *in my Vein* –
But *He* must *count the drops* – *himself* –
*My price* for *every stain*!

c. 1862

One need not be a Chamber — to be
    Haunted —
One need not be a House —
The Brain has Corridors — surpassing
Material Place —

Far safer, of a Midnight Meeting
External Ghost
Than its interior Confronting —
That Cooler Host.

Far safer, through an Abbey gallop,
The Stones a'chase —
Than Unarmed, one's a'self encounter —
In lonesome Place —

Ourself behind ourself, concealed —
Should startle most —
Assassin hid in our Apartment
Be Horror's least.

The Body – borrows a Revolver –
He bolts the Door –
O'erlooking a superior spectre –
Or More –

c. 1863

THE Zeroes – taught us – Phosphorus –
We learned to like the Fire
By playing Glaciers – when a Boy –
And Tinder – guessed – by power
Of Opposite – to balance Odd –
If White – a Red – must be!
Paralysis – our Primer – dumb –
Unto Vitality!

c. 1863

A Thought went up my mind today –
That I have had before –
But did not finish – some way back –
I could not fix the Year –

Nor where it went – nor why it came
The second time to me –
Nor definitely, what it was –
Have I the Art to say –

But somewhere – in my Soul – I know –
I've met the Thing before –
It just reminded me – 'twas all –
And came my way no more –

c. 1863

Because I could not stop for Death –
He kindly stopped for me –
The Carriage held but just Ourselves –
And Immortality.

We slowly drove – He knew no haste
And I had put away
My labor and my leisure too,
For His Civility –

We passed the School, where Children
strove
At Recess – in the Ring –
We passed the Fields of Gazing Grain –
We passed the Setting Sun –

Or rather – He passed Us –
The Dews drew quivering and chill –
For only Gossamer, my Gown –
My Tippet – only Tulle –

We paused before a House that seemed
A Swelling of the Ground –
The Roof was scarcely visible –
The Cornice – in the Ground –

Since then – 'tis Centuries – and yet
Feels shorter than the Day
I first surmised the Horses' Heads
Were toward Eternity –

c. 1863

Publication – is the Auction
Of the Mind of Man –
Poverty – be justifying
For so foul a thing

Possibly – but We – would rather
From Our Garret go
White – Unto the White Creator –
Than invest – Our Snow –

Thought belong to Him who gave it –
Then – to Him Who bear
Its Corporeal illustration – Sell
The Royal Air –

In the Parcel – Be the Merchant
Of the Heavenly Grace –
But reduce no Human Spirit
To Disgrace of Price –

c. 1863

I MEANT to find Her when I came –
Death – had the same design –
But the Success – was His – it seems –
And the Surrender – Mine –

I meant to tell Her how I longed
For just this single time –
But Death had told Her so the first –
And she had past, with Him –

To wander – now – is my Repose –
To rest – To rest would be
A privilege of Hurricane
To Memory – and Me.

c. 1863

Behind Me – dips Eternity –
Before Me – Immortality –
Myself – the Term between –
Death but the Drift of Eastern Gray,
Dissolving into Dawn away,
Before the West begin –

'Tis Kingdoms – afterward – they say –
In perfect – pauseless Monarchy –
Whose Prince – is Son of None –
Himself – His Dateless Dynasty –
Himself – Himself diversify –
In Duplicate divine –

'Tis Miracle before Me – then –
'Tis Miracle behind – between –
A Crescent in the Sea –

With Midnight to the North of Her —
And Midnight to the South of Her —
And Maelstrom — in the Sky —

c. 1863

My Life had stood – a Loaded Gun –
In Corners – till a Day
The Owner passed – identified –
And carried Me away –

And now We roam in Sovereign Woods –
And now We hunt the Doe –
And every time I speak for Him –
The Mountains straight reply –

And do I smile, such cordial light
Upon the Valley glow –
It is as a Vesuvian face
Had let its pleasure through –

And when at Night – Our good Day
    done –
I guard My Master's Head –
'Tis better than the Eider-Duck's
Deep Pillow – to have shared –

_o foe of His — I'm deadly foe —
None stir the second time —
On whom I lay a Yellow Eye —
Or an emphatic Thumb —

Though I than He — may longer live
He longer must — than I —
For I have but the power to kill,
Without — the power to die —

c. 1863

Joy to have merited the Pain —
To merit the Release —
Joy to have perished every step —
To Compass Paradise —

Pardon — to look upon thy face —
With these old fashioned Eyes —
Better than new — could be — for that —
Though bought in Paradise —

Because they looked on thee before —
And thou hast looked on them —
Prove Me — My Hazel Witnesses
The features are the same —

So fleet thou wert, when present —
So infinite — when gone —
An Orient's Apparition —
Remanded of the Morn —

The Height I recollect —
'Twas even with the Hills —
The Depth upon my Soul was notched —
As Floods — on Whites of Wheels —

To Haunt — till Time have dropped
His last Decade away,
And Haunting actualize — to last
At least — Eternity —

c. 1863

THIS Consciousness that is aware
Of Neighbors and the Sun
Will be the one aware of Death
And that itself alone

Is traversing the interval
Experience between
And most profound experiment
Appointed unto Men —

How adequate unto itself
Its properties shall be
Itself unto itself and none
Shall make discovery.

Adventure most unto itself
The Soul condemned to be —
Attended by a single Hound
Its own identity.

c. 1864

Split the Lark — and you'll find the
    Music —
Bulb after Bulb, in Silver rolled —
Scantily dealt to the Summer Morning
Saved for your Ear when Lutes be old.

Loose the Flood — you shall find it
    patent —
Gush after Gush, reserved for you —
Scarlet Experiment! Sceptic Thomas!
Now, do you doubt that your Bird was
    true?

c. 1864

I STEPPED from Plank to Plank
A slow and cautious way
The Stars about my Head I felt
About my Feet the Sea.

I knew not but the next
Would be my final inch –
This gave me that precarious Gait
Some call Experience.

c. 1864

Faith – is the Pierless Bridge
Supporting what We see
Unto the Scene that We do not –
Too slender for the eye

It bears the Soul as bold
As it were rocked in Steel
With Arms of Steel at either side –
It joins – behind the Veil

To what, could We presume
The Bridge would cease to be
To Our far, vacillating Feet
A first Necessity.

c. 1864

STRUCK, was I, not yet by Lightning –
Lightning – lets away
Power to perceive His Process
With Vitality.

Maimed – was I – yet not by Venture –
Stone of stolid Boy –
Nor a Sportsman's Peradventure –
Who mine Enemy?

Robbed – was I – intact to Bandit –
All my Mansion torn –
Sun – withdrawn to Recognition –
Furthest shining – done –

Yet was not the foe – of any –
Not the smallest Bird
In the nearest Orchard dwelling
Be of Me – afraid.

Most — I love the Cause that slew Me.
Often as I die
Its beloved Recognition
Holds a Sun on Me —

Best — at Setting — as is Nature's —
Neither witnessed Rise
Till the infinite Aurora
In the other's eyes.

c. 1864

I FELT a Cleaving in my Mind —
As if my Brain had split —
I tried to match it — Seam by Seam —
But could not make them fit.

The thought behind, I strove to join
Unto the thought before —
But Sequence ravelled out of Sound
Like Balls — upon a Floor.

c. 1864

Under the Light, yet under,
Under the Grass and the Dirt,
Under the Beetle's Cellar
Under the Clover's Root,

Further than Arm could stretch
Were it Giant long,
Further than Sunshine could
Were the Day Year long,

Over the Light, yet over,
Over the Arc of the Bird —
Over the Comet's chimney —
Over the Cubit's Head,

Further than Guess can gallop
Further than Riddle ride —
Oh for a Disc to the Distance
Between Ourselves and the Dead!

c. 1864

THE Missing All – prevented Me
From missing minor Things.
If nothing larger than a World's
Departure from a Hinge –
Or Sun's extinction, be observed –
'Twas not so large that I
Could lift my Forehead from my work
For Curiosity.

c. 1865

I NEVER saw a Moor —
I never saw the Sea —
Yet know I how the Heather looks
And what a Billow be.

I never spoke with God
Nor visited in Heaven —
Yet certain am I of the spot
As if the Checks were given —

c. 1865

A NARROW Fellow in the Grass
Occasionally rides –
You may have met Him – did you not
His notice sudden is –

The Grass divides as with a Comb –
A spotted shaft is seen –
And then it closes at your feet
And opens further on –

He likes a Boggy Acre
A Floor too cool for Corn –
Yet when a Boy, and Barefoot –
I more than once at Noon
Have passed, I thought, a Whip lash
Unbraiding in the Sun
When stooping to secure it
It wrinkled, and was gone –

Several of Nature's People
I know, and they know me —
I feel for them a transport
Of cordiality —

But never met this Fellow
Attended, or alone
Without a tighter breathing
And Zero at the Bone —

c. 1865

THERE is a Zone whose even Years
No Solstice interrupt –
Whose Sun constructs perpetual Noon
Whose perfect Seasons wait –

Whose Summer set in Summer, till
The Centuries of June
And Centuries of August cease
And Consciousness – is Noon.

c. 1865

THE last Night that She lived
It was a Common Night
Except the Dying – this to Us
Made Nature different

We noticed smallest things –
Things overlooked before
By this great light upon our Minds
Italicized – as 'twere.

As We went out and in
Between Her final Room
And Rooms where Those to be alive
Tomorrow were, a Blame

That Others could exist
While She must finish quite
A Jealousy for Her arose
So nearly infinite –

We waited while She passed —
It was a narrow time —
Too jostled were Our Souls to speak
At length the notice came.

She mentioned, and forgot —
Then lightly as a Reed
Bent to the Water, struggled scarce —
Consented, and was dead —

And We — We placed the Hair —
And drew the Head erect —
And then an awful leisure was
Belief to regulate —

c. 1866

Tell all the Truth but tell it slant —
Success in Circuit lies
Too bright for our infirm Delight
The Truth's superb surprise

As Lightning to the Children eased
With explanation kind
The Truth must dazzle gradually
Or every man be blind —

c. 1868

THE Wind took up the Northern Things
And piled them in the south —
Then gave the East unto the West
And opening his mouth

The four Divisions of the Earth
Did make as to devour
While everything to corners slunk
Behind the awful power —

The Wind — unto his Chambers went
And nature ventured out —
Her subjects scattered into place
Her systems ranged about

Again the smoke from Dwellings rose
The Day abroad was heard —
How intimate, a Tempest past
The Transport of the Bird —

c. 1868

THE Life we have is very great.
The Life that we shall see
Surpasses it, we know, because
It is Infinity.
But when all Space has been beheld
And all Dominion shown
The smallest Human Heart's extent
Reduces it to none.

1870

SAFE Despair it is that raves —
Agony is frugal.
Puts itself severe away
For its own perusal.

Garrisoned no Soul can be
In the Front of Trouble —
Love is one, not aggregate —
Nor is Dying double —

c. 1873

Wonder — is not precisely Knowing
And not precisely Knowing not —
A beautiful but bleak condition
He has not lived who has not felt —

Suspense — is his maturer Sister —
Whether Adult Delight is Pain
Or of itself a new misgiving —
This is the Gnat that mangles men —

c. 1874

It sounded as if the Streets were running
And then — the Streets stood still —
Eclipse — was all we could see at the
   Window
And Awe — was all we could feel.

By and by — the boldest stole out of his
   Covert
To see if Time was there —
Nature was in an Opal Apron,
Mixing fresher Air.

c. 1877

To see the Summer Sky
Is Poetry, though never in a Book it lie —
True Poems flee —

c. 1879

Fame is the one that does not stay —
Its occupant must die
Or out of sight of estimate
Ascend incessantly —
Or be that most insolvent thing
A Lightning in the Germ —
Electrical the embryo
But we demand the Flame

c. 1879

Apparently with no surprise
To any happy Flower
The Frost beheads it at its play –
In accidental power –
The blonde Assassin passes on –
The Sun proceeds unmoved
To measure off another Day
For an Approving God.

c. 1884

THE pedigree of Honey
Does not concern the Bee,
Nor lineage of Ecstasy
Delay the Butterfly
On spangled journeys to the peak
Of some perceiveless thing —
The right of way to Tripoli
A more essential thing.

version I
c. 1884

THE Pedigree of Honey
Does not concern the Bee –
A Clover, any time, to him,
Is Aristocracy –

version II
c. 1884

M<small>Y</small> life closed twice before its close —
It yet remains to see
If Immortality unveil
A third event to me

So huge, so hopeless to conceive
As these that twice befell.
Parting is all we know of heaven,
And all we need of hell.

[date unknown]

THE reticent volcano keeps
His never slumbering plan —
Confided are his projects pink
To no precarious man.

If nature will not tell the tale
Jehovah told to her
Can human nature not survive
Without a listener?

Admonished by her buckled lips
Let every babbler be
The only secret people keep
Is Immortality.

[date unknown]

# AFTERWORD

The literature that survives for many generations is handed down as dutifully as each generation is able to manage the transfer. In the case of Dickinson's work, the early editors made such egregious mistakes that we are likely only to improve the situation, though we may certainly make our own errors. The poems have been rendered and loved in so many editions that we must conclude that they will shine no matter what.

I have chosen to use the versions of the poems edited by Thomas H. Johnson; these are the most widely read at the present time. Johnson worked from Dickinson's original manuscripts and sought to restore much of her original punctuation and lineation after it had been changed and standardized by some of her earlier editors; he also tried to restore the original capitalizations. In his edition of 1955, he reproduced her spelling errors as he found them, but in subsequent volumes, he standardized the spellings of most words (except the proper names). Since the poems are taught and anthologized most frequently with the corrected spellings, I have made the decision to follow Johnson's instinct in this matter as well.

The reader should note, however, that there is controversy about how the lineations of the poems might appear if Dickinson herself had been able to see these poems in print. Some important scholarship is being done on the question of whether she wanted to be "consistent" with her quatrains, or whether the poems were meant to be lineated in a much less regular way than the versions we have. Since there are such irregularities in Dickinson's handwriting, there is no way of knowing whether she intended to use the same stanzaic structures, and I see no possible way of settling the matter. The only versions we have from her are the original manuscripts, which are available in facsimile editions; I refer the interested reader to those for further study.

# INDEX OF FIRST LINES

# INDEX OF FIRST LINES

LIBRARY OF CONGRESS
CATALOGING-IN-PUBLICATION DATA

Dickinson, Emily, 1830–1886.
[Poems. Selections]
The pocket Emily Dickinson / Emily Dickinson;
edited by Brenda Hillman.
p.   cm.
Previously published as: Poems. 1995.
Includes index.
ISBN 978-1-59030-700-7 (pbk.: acid-free paper)
I. Hillman, Brenda.   II. Title.
PS1541.A6   2009
811'.4—dc22
2008047327

*(Continued on next page)*